SCOTLAND
A PICTURE MEMORY

Text
Bill Harris

Captions
Nicola Dent

Design
Teddy Hartshorn

Photography
Colour Library Books Ltd.
Tom Till

Editorial
David Gibbon

Production
Ruth Arthur
Sally Connolly
Neil Randles

Director of Production
Gerald Hughes

CLB 2522
© 1993 CLB Publishing, Godalming, Surrey
This 1993 edition published by Magna Books,
Magna Road, Wigston, Leicester LE18 4ZH
Printed and bound in Singapore.
ISBN 1-85422-525-1

SCOTLAND
A PICTURE MEMORY

MAGNA BOOKS

Toward the end of every summer, the hottest news in most places usually concerns the length of skirt women will be wearing in the fall. In Scotland, however, it is more likely to be the length of the summer itself that is debated. Predictably, it will have been short. As for skirts, there is never any question about how long *they* ought to be, it has been the same for generations – at least for the variety that the men wear. A man's kilt must just graze the floor when he is kneeling; any other length just won't do. Traditionally, the kilt is made of seven yards of tartan, a woolen fabric, which allows for the pleating and is the secret of its warmth. The pleats are sewn in place at the top, but the bottom is not hemmed. It is a wrap-around garment, plain in front and fastened at the side with a massive silver pin. The kilt is never confused with a skirt, except outside Scotland, because, make no mistake, a Scotsman in his kilt is no softie dressed like a girl. The Highlanders who invented them were among the fiercest fighters ever to march into battle.

Both the Ancient Egyptians and the Greeks wore kilt-like garments, but the Scots didn't discover their advantages until about two hundred years ago. Before then, Highlanders relied on a sixteen-yard piece of tartan, called a plaid, that served as a blanket and doubled as a suit. To make the conversion it was necessary to lie the fabric on the ground, fold it into pleats, lie down on top of it, gather it around the body and secure it with a wide belt. It was a complicated process, and by the time a soldier was dressed for battle it was probably time for lunch. Eventually someone had the bright idea of cutting the plaid in half and making it into a kilt, thus reducing dressing time even more.

The Romans tried to conquer the tribes in the north of Great Britain but never quite succeeded, though they did captivate them with an odd musical instrument which they had inherited from the Greeks. This consisted of an air-filled bladder that discharged through reeds to make a musical sound that takes some getting used to. However, it didn't take the Celtic peoples in both Scotland and Ireland very long to claim it as their own. In Scotland especially, the pipes became a status symbol among clan chiefs, none of whom considered their retinue complete without a personal bagpiper. Outsiders claim that the warlike Highlanders ran all the more speedily into battle to escape the shrieking pipes, but they themselves claimed that bagpipe music stirred their souls and inspired fear in their enemies. It may be true. Even today the bagpipes are regarded with great affection among the Scottish.

And there are plenty of transplanted Scotsmen to share the emotion. The population of Scotland itself is less than that of New York City, but it has been estimated that there are some twenty million of her emigrant sons and daughters scattered around the world. That's more people than live in all of New York State, which is about the same size as Scotland. But, though many of them have no intention of ever going back to stay, not one of them has any thought of going back on their heritage. They may live in Nova Scotia or New Zealand, but their hearts are still, as they say, in the Highlands. The fact that their roots are just as likely to be in the Lowlands and that many may never actually have seen the Old Country doesn't detract from their sincerity.

The world is full of people who have abandoned their roots, but almost all of them have done so to escape oppression, persecution or starvation. Not so the Scots. Their history has had its share of bloody conflict, but they've never been an oppressed or persecuted people. Famine has never been a factor, either, and though the climate may sometimes leave something to be desired, the Scots have thrived in places that make John o' Groats seem like a summer resort. They seem equally at home in steaming jungles and hostile deserts, but even those who have settled in places that resemble their native land know in their hearts that no other place matches Scotland for natural beauty.

It seems likely that when people begin living in space stations one of the first things they will do is form a St. Andrew's Society. Not only that, but the Burns Society will still insist on having haggis, freshly made and not freeze-dried, for its annual banquet, and there will be caber tossing and hammer throwing at the ultimate "Highland" games. The precedent has already been established. Neil Armstrong, the first man on the moon, though technically an American, was really a Scotsman in disguise.

It's been said that the migrations, which began well before other Europeans began exploring the world, are a direct result of a natural curiosity and love of adventure. But there was a profit motive, too. Some of the first Scots to leave home were merchants who carried furs across the North Sea and engaged in history's first price wars. Their competitors threw up their hands and claimed that they couldn't afford to operate on such slim profit margins. Thus the legend of Scottish thrift was born. But there were other Scottish qualities that would become legendary, too. When a population explosion in the seventeenth century forced as many as a hundred thousand of Scotland's young men to migrate to continental Europe, nearly all of them became soldiers. By the time the English began expanding their interests abroad, Highland regiments had already fought in the armies of Sweden, France, Holland and Prussia, and a Scotsman had founded the Russian Navy. Years later, John Paul Jones, a native of Kirkudbright, founded the American Navy.

When Scotland's King James VI became James I of England in 1603, he took his own men along with him to London, thus giving rise to another legend – that of the Scots as natural-born administrators. But it was as soldiers that they were most admired. Compared with other European powers, however, the English were late in taking advantage of this resource. The first Highland regiment in the English army consisted of half a dozen independent companies of military police that had seen service in Scotland before going south in the 1740s. They were identified by a dark tartan, which gave them the name "Black Watch." Within a dozen years, additional companies were added to create a regiment of a thousand men. The Black Watch first saw action against the French at Fontenoy in 1745. The French forces won the day, but the Scotsmen earned a reputation for fearlessness in attack and for coolness and patience in retreat. Over the next half-century, nearly thirty-five Highland regiments were formed, some of which are still the pride of the British army. William Pitt, the Earl of Chatham, took most of the credit: "I sought for merit wherever it was to be found," he told Parliament. "It is my boast that I was the first minister who looked for it and found it in the mountains of the North. I called it forth and drew it into your service ... they fought with valour and conquered for you in every part of the world."

Rhetoric aside, the Highlanders are possibly the greatest natural soldiers in the world, being stubborn defenders and daring attackers. Yet they're an equally remarkable breed out of battle dress. They have a personal code of honor that makes crime virtually unknown, and a loyalty to each other that seems impossible to shake. These qualities make for good police officers, and though Americans tend to think of Ireland as the best source of law-enforcers, the Royal Candian Mounted Police owes its reputation to the Scotsmen in its ranks. Equally, although the English would deny it, London's Metropolitan Police get their high marks from bobbies with Scottish backgrounds, though the name "Scotland Yard" has nothing to do with it.

It's an odd name for a police department, but one which has been with us for a thousand years. History tells of a plot of land in London that was granted to a Scottish king as a base, should he ever want to visit the English court. He didn't, nor did many of his successors, but the grant was perpetuated as a little bit of Scotland on the Thames. Eventually, the expanding English bureaucracy put an office building on the land, which finally became the headquarters of the police department when that was established in the 1820s. By that point, Scotland had become part of the United Kingdom and no one questioned taking back the original gift.

The Union took place in 1707, or so the treaty says. But bringing the Scots into the fold took a good bit longer. They are not an easy race to subdue.

The Romans were the first to try, attacking the northeast during their occupation of Britain. Possibly because of the weather, which they mentioned frequently in their journals, or more likely because of the natives, they didn't stay very long. They encountered a race of men they called "Picti" who painted their bodies blue, wore shaggy furs and were handy with heavy clubs. The legions had conquered more savage people, but the ones we now call Picts managed to keep them at arm's length and, probably grumbling about the fog and mist, the Romans turned tail and went back south. They tried again about fifty years later, persevering for another forty years, during which time they built a line of forts and a wall between the Forth and Clyde rivers. After they withdrew, there was a third attempt to include the Picts in the Roman Empire, but that didn't work out either, and the land was ready for invasion by the Christians.

They weren't long in coming. In the meantime, immigrants, who called themselves Scots, began arriving from Ireland. The Picts, a dark-haired race, began intermarrying with the sandy-haired, fair-skinned newcomers and, along with the Vikings who had moved in from the north, created something new: the Scotsman. In the middle of the sixth century, a Christian missionary called Columba arrived from Ireland and established an outpost on the island of Iona from which to spread the Gospel on the mainland. Thanks to him, the Scots became Christians. In another three hundred years, the four separate kingdoms, apparently fed up with fighting among themselves, became one, which they named Scotland. The Norsemen were still holding parts of the mainland and many of the northern islands, but the Scots, under King Duncan I, were more interested in sacking English castles and in defending their own against vengeful Englishmen.

Duncan was the king Macbeth murdered to gain the throne for himself. Then Macbeth was killed, Malcolm III succeeded him and Scotland was never the same again. Actually, it was Malcolm's wife, Margaret, who changed things. She had been an English princess and never let go her English ways. She loved England and she loved the English church even more, changing the Celtic church she found in Scotland into something more like it. In addition to importing English-speaking clergy, she anglicized her husband's court and raised her sons in the traditions she had loved as a girl. Three of them became kings themselves and continued the transformation of Scotland into a feudal kingdom that was a carbon copy of Norman England.

Though they didn't object to annexing Northumbria, the Scots had no intention of becoming English. The English king disabused them of that notion and forced his northern neighbors to pay him homage. This continued for about fifteen years, until Richard the Lionheart let them go their separate ways in gratitude for their contribution to his crusade. During the next decades, they concentrated on ousting the Norsemen. Then, in 1286, King Alexander III died, leaving his throne to his baby granddaughter Margaret, the Maid of Norway. This prompted both John Balliol and Robert Bruce to stake claims to the throne, but a council of nobility and clergy voted for Margaret. This choice was confirmed by England's King Edward I, who arranged a marriage between Margaret and his son – even though Margaret was only three years old and her grandmother was Edward's sister. The plan was foiled when Margaret died. In order to avert a civil war, Edward appointed himself overlord of Scotland and made Balliol his surrogate. But Balliol decided he didn't need any help from London, forcing Edward to meet, and defeat, the Scots in battle, destroy their great seal and move the symbolic Stone of Scone, which had been used in Scottish coronations for six hundred years, into his own court.

It was only a matter of time before the Scots reacted. In the uprising that followed, Robert Bruce declared himself King of Scotland, but it took him seven years of fighting, both against other Scots and the English, to make the idea stick. Finally, after defeating the English at Bannockburn, his claim was affirmed and Scotland was once again an independent nation.

Bruce lived only two years after that, and the crown soon passed to his kinsmen, the Stewarts. Thus began two centuries of war and intrigue. By the time Mary Stewart became the Queen of Scots, the Protestant Reformation had swept both England and Scotland, taking the form of Episcopalianism in the former and of Presbyterianism in the latter. Mary had a stronger claim to England's throne than its then occupier: Elizabeth I. However, Mary, being a catholic, was out of step on both sides of the border. After being forced to abdicate and then to spend twenty years in an English prison, she was beheaded.

When Queen Elizabeth I died, James VI of Scotland became James I of England, but the two countries didn't unite and for the next 150 years religious quarrels kept the Scots at each other's throats. In 1688, when James II was deposed for his papist leanings, the Highlands rocked with a rebellion that culminated in the defeat of Prince Charles Edward, fondly remembered as Bonnie Prince Charlie, at Culloden in 1745. It was the last battle fought on British soil, and it marked the end of the old Highland way of life. The English made the wearing of kilts, or any tartan for that matter, illegal, as well as banning bagpipes and disarming the clans. By the mid-nineteenth century the Highlands were virtually empty.

The old symbols were reinstated in the 1820s; then, in the 1860s, Queen Victoria built Balmoral Castle and pronounced it her favorite place. It was a signal that all was forgiven. Well, nearly all. You can still get into a friendly discussion in a Glasgow pub over the differences between the Scots and the English. You might get some new insight into why both groups don't habitually call themselves British, although Scotland's and England's parliaments have long been amalgamated into one legislative body that unites them under that name. Maybe some day they will. The merger was made in 1707 but some people on either side of the border haven't got used to it yet. It didn't even seem strange when, back in 1858, it was officially ruled that these people who had been calling themselves "Scotch" for centuries should henceforth be known as Scottish. Scotch, it was pointed out then, and will be repeated to you today if you should misuse the term, is a type of whisky and not the definition of a people.

Parliaments notwithstanding, just as there'll always be an England, so there will always be a Scotland. It took so many centuries to develop the national character, we'll probably never see the day when the Scots and the English will both answer to no other name than British. If they were to, how would Scotland's ghosts take it? They say that Bonnie Prince Charlie still roams Culloden Moor and that the fourteenth-century Battle of Killiecrankie between the MacDonalds and the MacLeods is often refought on dark nights. Lady Anne Douglas, who has been dead for centuries, is regularly seen, with her head tucked under her arm, of course, at Drumlanrig. At Glamis Castle, where Macbeth murdered Duncan, locals swear that a centuries-old, once-human monster can still be heard scratching around behind a bricked-over door – cursing his fate in Gaelic, no doubt. Old traditions die hard in Scotland.

One that will never die, at least as long as the tourist trade exists, is the Loch Ness monster. She (yes, of course, *she*) was first noted by St. Columba more than fourteen centuries ago. He told the Picts that a water monster would get them if they didn't watch their step. People have been watching the loch for a sight of the beastie ever since. Some say they've seen her, and up around Inverness they claim that some lucky tourist is likely to get a photograph of her any day now. Is there a monster? Loch Ness is twice as deep as the North Sea, of which it was once a part, and if there was ever an environment suited to a sea monster, Loch Ness is surely it. But, like Scotland itself, her story is shrouded in mist. And, also like Scotland, she has to be seen to be believed. There may not be another romantic setting in all the world comparable to the northern end of Great Britain, and no setting has inspired more legends than Scotland, a country where anything seems possible.

Facing page: the ruins of Castle Kennedy, encircled by charming gardens and standing on a peninsula between two lochs near Stranraer.

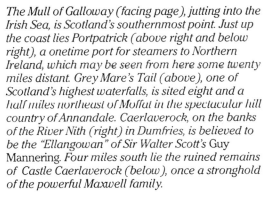

The Mull of Galloway (facing page), jutting into the Irish Sea, is Scotland's southernmost point. Just up the coast lies Portpatrick (above right and below right), a onetime port for steamers to Northern Ireland, which may be seen from here some twenty miles distant. Grey Mare's Tail (above), one of Scotland's highest waterfalls, is sited eight and a half miles northeast of Moffat in the spectacular hill country of Annandale. Caerlaverock, on the banks of the River Nith (right) in Dumfries, is believed to be the "Ellangowan" of Sir Walter Scott's Guy Mannering. Four miles south lie the ruined remains of Castle Caerlaverock (below), once a stronghold of the powerful Maxwell family.

The Firth of Forth is spanned by bridges (left and below) for both road and rail traffic; the latter is of cantilevered construction and was completed in 1890. The Palace of Holyroodhouse (above) is Scotland's premier royal residence and its magnificent state apartments are regularly stayed in by the Queen of England. Beautiful Abbotsford House (facing page top) was the home, inspiration and death place of novelist Sir Walter Scott. Galashiels (facing page bottom) is a tweed- and woolen-producing town in a picturesque valley in the Borders.

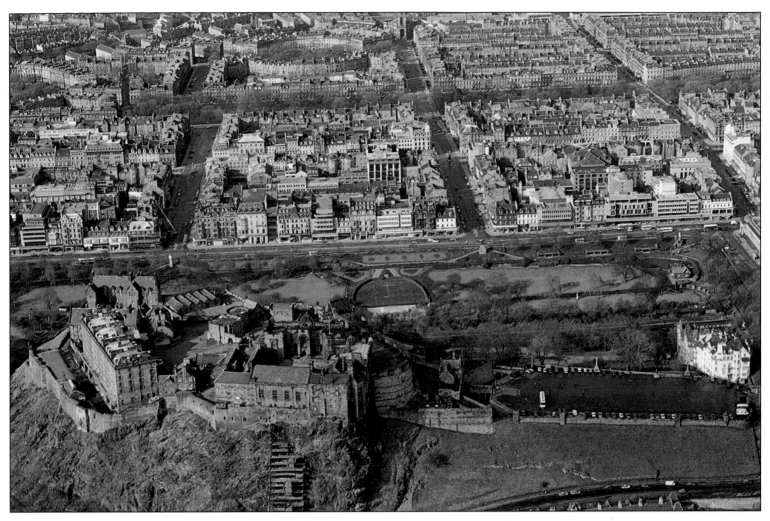

Edinburgh (these pages), Scotland's capital since 1437, has a grand and important heritage that has left its unmistakable imprint on its people and buildings. Many famous people have lived in and loved Edinburgh, including the religious reformer John Knox, whose house (right) may be found on the Royal Mile. Above and below: the spectacularly situated castle.

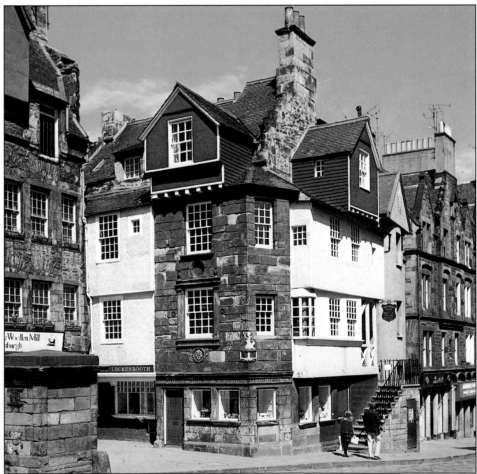

Annual events in Edinburgh (these pages) include the internationally acclaimed Military Tattoo (above), performed in front of the floodlit castle (facing page), and the International Festival of the Arts, which is accompanied with fireworks of all kinds. Below: the Royal Scots Greys Memorial. Right: traditional pipers.

17

Culzean Castle (left), facing Culzean Bay between Ayr and Girvan, dates mainly from 1777, though one tower is of earlier construction. It is one of Robert Adam's finest creations and is situated in delightful grounds which, like the house, are open to the public during the summer months. From the Brig O' Doon in Alloway, Ayr, may be seen a memorial (below) to Robert Burns, the man who immortalized the bridge in his poem "Tam o' Shanter." The son of a farmer, Burns pursued an agricultural career himself for a time, though this proved unsuccessful and Burns finally became an exciseman in Dumfries. The literati of Edinburgh society took the young poet to their hearts and his patron, the Earl of Glencairn, saw to it that the Caledonian Hunt paid for the publishing of his second book of poems. Sadly, Burns met a premature death after contracting rheumatic fever following a night spent sleeping by a Dumfries roadside after a heavy drinking bout. A statue (facing page bottom) of Scotland's great bard stands in well-manicured gardens off Beresford Terrace in the town of Ayr, with which he is closely associated. The romantic ruins of Kilchurn Castle (facing page top) stand on raised ground which was once an island in Upper Loch Awe. Built by Sir Colin Campbell, Knight of Rhodes, the oldest parts of the castle date back to 1440.

Glasgow, on the River Clyde, is one of the biggest cities in the British Isles, and contains Scotland's biggest seaport. Clydeside has a long tradition as a shipbuilding center, though many of the yards are shut down today. Other local industries include textiles, engineering and chemicals. Glasgow is a cultural center too, and boasts many fine galleries and grand public buildings. Right: the City Chambers on George Square, (below right) the University on Gilmorehill, and (bottom right) the Gothic-style Glasgow Art Gallery and Museum. Below: the setting sun softens the silhouettes of industrial machinery on the banks of the Clyde beyond Kingston Bridge. Also situated on the Firth of Clyde, and of importance to Scotland's shipbuilding industry, is Greenock, a town much damaged during the Second World War. A distinctive cross of Lorraine (left), on Lyle Hill, commemorates the French sailors who lost their lives in the Battle of the Atlantic.

The west coast of Scotland is a popular place among the yachting fraternity; its many resort towns offer great opportunities for the keen sailor. Prominent among the picturesque sea ports are Gourock (above), on the Rosneath Peninsula, with its pebble beach and pier, and Crinan (left), with its charming harbor. The triple peaks of the Paps of Jura may be seen from Port Askaig (top right) on the Isle of Islay, from where ferries depart for Jura itself. The Paps are each around 2,500 feet in height and provide excellent vantage points from which to view other glorious Inner Hebridean Islands such as Colonsay and Oronsay. Off the north coast of Jura, over the Strait of Corryvreckan, lies another small island, called Scarba. Although not far apart, a powerful whirlpool prohibits traffic between the two. Dunoon (above right), another of Argyll's beauty spots, features a statue of Burns' sweetheart, Mary Campbell, looking out over the Firth of Clyde from Castle Hill. Mary's precipitate death put paid to the couple's intentions to marry and emigrate to Jamaica after Burns' first published work, Poems, Chiefly in the Scottish Dialect, proved a great success in 1786. Largs (right) is a Clyde coast yachting resort sheltered by surrounding hills that reach 1,700 feet in height.

Magnificent seascapes and island scenery attract holidaymakers to the resort of Oban, where the harbor (below, right and facing page) is alive with fishing boats, ferries, yachts and steamers, and trips depart from the bay for the Inner Hebridean Islands across the Firth of Lorne. Of unique interest is McCaig's folly, a huge stone structure resembling the Colosseum in Rome which perches on a hill overlooking the bay. The project, which was never completed, was begun in 1897 by a benevolent local banker who sought to make use of the town's craftsmen during a slump. South of Oban lies the small slate-quarrying island of Easdale (above).

26

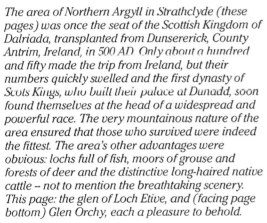

The area of Northern Argyll in Strathclyde (these pages) was once the seat of the Scottish Kingdom of Dalriada, transplanted from Dunsererick, County Antrim, Ireland, in 500 AD. Only about a hundred and fifty made the trip from Ireland, but their numbers quickly swelled and the first dynasty of Scots Kings, who built their palace at Dunadd, soon found themselves at the head of a widespread and powerful race. The very mountainous nature of the area ensured that those who survived were indeed the fittest. The area's other advantages were obvious: lochs full of fish, moors of grouse and forests of deer and the distinctive long-haired native cattle – not to mention the breathtaking scenery. This page: the glen of Loch Etive, and (facing page bottom) Glen Orchy, each a pleasure to behold.

Inverary Castle (top left and below) is the seat of the Dukes of Argyll, chiefs of the Clan Campbell, and has been since the fifteenth century. On his tour of the Highlands in 1773, Dr. Johnson stayed in the castle at the invitation of the Fifth Duke. Castle Stalker (right), the ancient home of the Stewarts of Appin, sits prettily on a tiny island in Loch Laich. Built around 1500, the castle is linked with King James IV and bears the Royal Arms over its entrance. As the snows of winter are melted by the spring sun, so the myriad rivers of the Highlands fill with rushing, crystal-clear water. Above left: Black Mount, (below left) Kingshouse Hotel, on the River Etive, and (above) the River Beathach, Glen Orchy.

The old county of Perthshire (these pages), which contained both the forested Trossachs region and the Grampian Mountains, was one of Scotland's loveliest counties. Robert the Bruce lost his brooch during a battle near Tyndrum (above) in 1306 and it may be seen on show in the Macdougall mansion nearby. Balquhidder, on romantic Loch Voil, is best-known as the burial place of "Rob Roy" MacGregor, the Robin Hood of the north, who died in 1734. Facing page top: Killin, a picturesque resort on the River Dochart (below and facing page bottom).

Stirling (above), the gateway to the Highlands, is a famous old Royal Burgh situated on a loop of the River Forth. Its magnificent castle (right) stands overlooking the fields on which the Battle of Bannockburn was fought in 1314. Scottish monarchs have been born, crowned and met their deaths within the castle's walls; in 1543 Mary, Queen of Scots was made Queen in its church, at the age of nine months. Below: Castle Campbell, near the Burn of Care; (facing page bottom) the River Leny; and (facing page top) Loch Ard, southeast of Ben Lomond.

Fife (these pages) is famous as the home of golf;
the Royal and Ancient Golf Club (right) at St.
Andrews is the foremost club in the world and the
ruling authority on the game. In 1160, twenty years
after St. Andrews was established as a Royal Burgh,
work began on a Cathedral, the ruins of which
(above and below) are an impressive sight. Facing
page top: Pittenweem Harbor and (facing page
bottom) Anstruther, crowned with a rainbow.

35

The "Fair City" of Perth (above and right), once the capital of Scotland, stands at the head of the estuary of the River Tay among glorious countryside of hills and meadows. Perth is steeped in history, having been taken by Cromwell in 1651 and then occupied during the Jacobite uprisings of 1715 and 1745. The city's architecture and historic buildings are all part of its heritage and lend an auspicious air to this already atmospheric place. Like St. Andrews, the area around Perth is a great golfing center – the courses at Gleneagles (above left) being synonymous with the top end of the game. Picturesque Crieff (top left) nestles on a hillside above Strath Earn in Tayside. Three miles south lies Drummond Castle (left), the site of more of Cromwell's bombardments – little more than the tower containing the armory is original. The neat landscaped gardens are open to the public.

Tayside is characterized by magnificent wooded scenery and extensive lochs which have earnt it the praise of many different visitors. Queen Victoria herself was enchanted by the view from a spot upon the north bank of Loch Tummel (below left) which takes in snow-capped Shiehallion and Loch Rannoch (facing page bottom). Furthermore, Burns was moved to render in verse his impression of the view of Loch Tay to be had from the stone bridge (above left) at Kenmore. East of Loch Rannoch, Loch Faskally (facing page top) has been created by constructing a fifty-four-foot-high dam at Pitlochry as part of the area's hydroelectric scheme. The River Bran (left) is a pretty picture viewed from the bridges near the cathedral city of Dunkeld, Tayside, while Aberfeldy (above) is carpeted with daffodils in the spring. Below: Blair Castle, near Blair Atholl, built by the Duke of Atholl in 1269.

Aberdeen (right and facing page bottom), as well as being a major university and cathedral city, is Scotland's largest fishing port and the capital of the North Sea oil industry. It is dubbed the "Silver City" because of the effect produced by the predominant use of granite in its construction, which also makes it one of the handsomest cities in the country. Aberdeen has literary associations too, boasting a statue of Lord Byron in front of its grammar school – though the famous poet recieved little praise in the country in which he was raised. A damning review of his first published work, Hours of Idleness (1807), which appeared in the Edinburgh Review, caused Byron to pen the satire English Bards and Scotch Reviewers. Aviemore (facing page top) is well known as a year-round Highland resort and is Britain's skiing center. Above: Findochty, a quaint fishing village on the rocky Grampian coast.

The Cairngorms, that extensive group of flat-topped mountains in the Highlands, are at their most majestic when tipped with snow. The Speyside resort of Newtonmore (facing page top) provides a good vantage point from which to take them in. Loch Moy is as well suited to the golden months of fall (facing page bottom) as to the silver tones of winter (above), while Loch Morlich (below) is enhanced by a setting sun. Loch Ness (left) is world famous for its much speculated upon but little seen monster!

43

Ben Nevis is Britain's highest mountain, standing 4,406 feet high, and seen for miles around, including from such vantage points as the Caledonian Canal (top left), Fort William (above) and Banavie (right and left). The Caledonian Canal effectively cuts Scotland in two, providing an at one time invaluable alternative to the sea trip around the treacherous Cape of Wrath for traffic destined for the opposite side of the country. A series of eight locks constructed at a tricky point along the canal's sixty-mile-length, near Banavie (left), is known as Neptune's Staircase. Snow adds a certain romance to the Highlands – for the visitor at any rate – and, encouraged by the frequent fogs, can remain in the crags of the mountains all year round. As part of the Lochaber energy sheme, a fifteen-mile-long pipe runs through Ben Nevis carrying water from Loch Treig near Tulloch (above left).

Lying in the Great Glen of the Highlands are Loch Unagin (above) and Loch Oich (facing page bottom), the northernmost of the lochs linked by the Caledonian Canal. Steamers, such as the King George V (left), ply the waters of the canal from Oban to Fort William during the summer months. Loch Leven (below left), east of Kinross, is a nature reserve and the site of a castle from which Mary, Queen of Scots, made a dramatic escape after a year's imprisonment therein. Her helper, a friend of the gaoler's son, is reputed to have thrown the keys into the loch – an event recorded in Sir Walter Scott's novel The Abbot. Glencoe (facing page top) is best known as the place where thirty-eight of the MacDonald clan met their deaths at the hands of Campbell of Glen Lyon and his soldiers.

These pages: the Pass of Glencoe, overshadowed by mountains and its sad history. The tragedy of the massacre in Glencoe lies in that those MacDonalds murdered for failing to swear allegiance to King William III of England, had in fact done so. The deadline for submission was January 1, 1692, and the MacDonalds of Glencoe, previously loyal to King James, offered their allegiance on December 31 at the local garrison. Confusion and delay, absent officials and time-consuming referrals conspired to result in the official submission not being received before troops had moved in to Glencoe on February 1; the orders for the massacre were received on February 12. The mountains of Dalness Forest include Buchaille Etive's twin peaks, near which lies a stone-built climbers' cottage (right). Facing page and below: the Glencoe River, cutting its way through the dramatic mountain pass (below right). Glencoe Pap overlooks a village (above right) and Loch Leven (above).

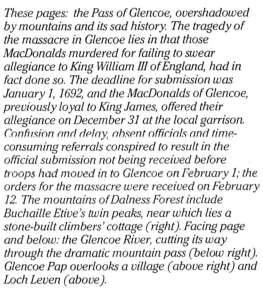

The busy port of Mallaig (facing page and below), on the northern shores of Morar in the Highland region, is a terminal for steamers to the Inner and Outer Hebridean Islands. On its way to Mallaig, the "Road to the Isles" passes through Glenfinnan, where the Prince Charles Edward monument (right) stands in a breathtaking spot overlooking the head of Loch Shiel. Erected in 1815, it marks the spot where Bonnie Prince Charlie raised his father's standard to mark the beginning of his attempt to recover the Stuart Crown in 1745. Above: nearby Loch Eilt.

The River Finnan is spanned by a railroad viaduct (right and below) just before the track reaches Glenfinnan station and the river empties into Loch Shiel. The great swooping curve of the bridge affords train travellers unforgettable views of Glen Finnan and beyond to the stony summit of Sgurr Thuilm and the twin peaks of the Streaps. Nearby Loch Eil (above and center left), overlooked by magnificent Ben Nevis, is plied by various boats. Above left: a bay near Morar and (bottom left) thirteenth-century Inverlochy Castle.

The Highland scenery of Glen Shiel (above left) so inspired Dr. Johnson when, in 1773, he rode through it on horseback, that he wrote Journey to the Western Isles in its praise. At the eastern end of the glen, beyond Loch Duich, rise the Five Sisters of Kintail (left), while to the west the Saddle (above) reaches a height of 3,317 feet. Driving along the windy, undulating Highland roads is almost as exciting an experience as is the anticipation as to what might be around the next corner or over the next hill ... vistas of unrivaled beauty amaze even the most indulged sightseer. Cresting a rise in the road bordering Loch Carron (below left) reveals that loch's myriad islands and gives an added edge to the sight of snow-tipped Beinn Eighe and Liathach towering in the background. Facing page and below: beautiful Eilean Donan Castle, built by Alexander II of Scotland in around 1220 and overlooking Loch Druich. It has suffered various attacks over the years, including a bombardment in the early eighteenth century by an English warship.

Named for an early King of Norway, Kyleakin (above, top right and below right), on the Isle of Skye (these pages), overlooks the narrow strait of Kyle Akin through which the King sailed on his journey to Largs in 1263. Castle Moil (below right) stands surveying the harbor but also affords a fine view up Loch Alsh, extending as far inland as the mountains of Kintail. Now ruined, the castle was for centuries a stronghold of the Mackinnons of Strath. Beyond the agricultural area of Tarksavaig (left and above right) rise the black Cuillin Mountains, cutting the Hebridean sky with their jagged peaks.

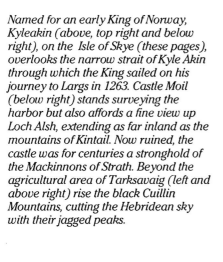

The western shore of the old, northern county of Ross and Cromarty (these pages) shelters many interesting little seaside towns, each with their stories to tell and each with a highly individual character. Highland hospitality is best savored in the sea-facing public houses, where the local whiskies are many and varied. Shieldaig (right), sheltered to the northeast by the great sandstone peaks of the Torridon Mountains, lies low on the shores of Loch Shieldag. The small community is involved in fishing and crofting, like that of Plockton (remaining pictures), part of the Balmacara Estate on Loch Carron. Plockton also affords views of the Torridon Mountains – some of which are topped with white quartzite – and also of the Applecross Mountains to the north.

The harvest of the sea has always been Scotland's bounty, and the Scots are great fishermen. Boats seem to crowd each and every one of the country's ports, their decks laden with the baskets, nets, ropes and floats of their trade. Sutherland boasts the ports of Kinlochbervie (left), in a peaceful setting on Loch Inchard, and Lochinver (below left), on the rocky coast of the Assynt district. Ullapool (right) and Wick (bottom left) are equally picturesque Highland ports. The northern coast is no place for small boats, however, being dangerous in the extreme with rocky outcrops such as Muckle and Little Stacks at Duncansby Head (below).

Some twenty miles beyond John O'Groats, across the Pentland Firth, are the Orkney Islands – about seventy in total, of which around twenty-eight are inhabited. The Orkneys, though tiny, have a significant and colorful history and have produced a surprising number of history-makers. The prohibitively tough conditions on the Islands may be the reason for the resilience, modesty and courage of its people. Many took the opportunity of a new life in Canada offered to them in the early 1770s and made good in the New World. One descendant of an Orkney immigrant who arrived in Nova Scotia in 1773 made it all the way to the top. His name was Ulysees Simpson Grant. The largest of the Orkney Islands, Mainland, features the remarkably intact neolithic village settlement of Skara Brae (above), just north of the fishing harbor at Stromness (facing page bottom). The Shetland Islands, further north still, are in fact closer to Norway than they are to England, reflected in the Island's place names and adopted Norse traditions. Their capital, Lerwick (facing page top), is a busy port on Mainland, as is Mid Yell (left) on the nearby island of Yell. Both groups of islands are known for their abundant and rare species of birdlife; the Shetlands are of course also famous for their tiny native ponies. Overleaf: a golden Scottish sunset over the North Sea.